Growing up Safe

Safety
in the home

Illustrated by Sue Wilkinson

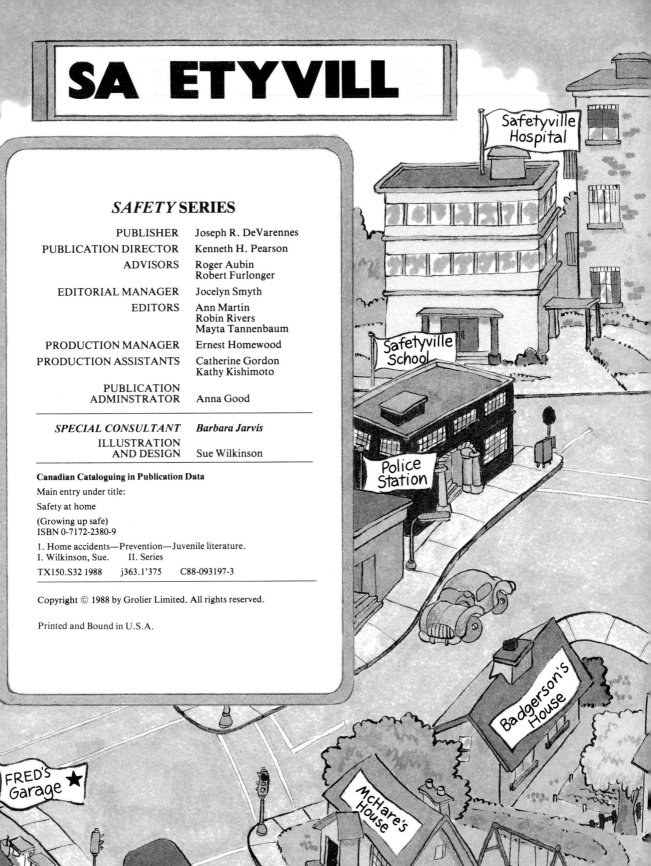

SA ETYVILL

SAFETY SERIES

PUBLISHER	Joseph R. DeVarennes
PUBLICATION DIRECTOR	Kenneth H. Pearson
ADVISORS	Roger Aubin
	Robert Furlonger
EDITORIAL MANAGER	Jocelyn Smyth
EDITORS	Ann Martin
	Robin Rivers
	Mayta Tannenbaum
PRODUCTION MANAGER	Ernest Homewood
PRODUCTION ASSISTANTS	Catherine Gordon
	Kathy Kishimoto
PUBLICATION ADMINSTRATOR	Anna Good

SPECIAL CONSULTANT	*Barbara Jarvis*
ILLUSTRATION AND DESIGN	Sue Wilkinson

Canadian Cataloguing in Publication Data

Main entry under title:

Safety at home

(Growing up safe)
ISBN 0-7172-2380-9

1. Home accidents—Prevention—Juvenile literature.
I. Wilkinson, Sue.   II. Series

TX150.S32 1988   j363.1'375   C88-093197-3

Safetyville Hospital

Safetyville School

Police Station

Badgerson's House

McHare's House

FRED'S Garage ★

Come join Kim, Timmy and Tina Badgerson as they find out everything they need to know about home safety.

BE CAREFUL OF CUPS THAT MAY CONTAIN HOT LIQUIDS.

Coffee, tea and soup can burn you.

NEVER PUT BUTTONS OR BEADS IN YOUR NOSE OR EARS.

DO NOT STAND ON BEDS OR CHAIRS.

STAIRS ARE NOT A SAFE PLACE
TO PLAY.

DO NOT TOUCH CONTAINERS WITH THIS SYMBOL.

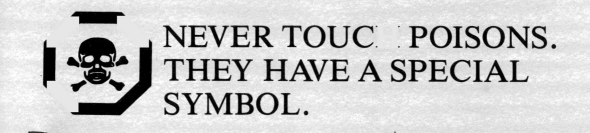

NEVER TOUCH POISONS.
THEY HAVE A SPECIAL
SYMBOL.

DO NOT PUT SMALL OBJECTS IN YOUR MOUTH.

KEEP YOUR FINGERS AND TOES AWAY FROM ANY PART OF A DOOR THAT IS CLOSING.

PUT TOYS AWAY—NEVER LEAVE THEM ON STAIRS.

I'll get Tina's wagon too.

A STOVE IS DANGEROUS.
THERE'S ALWAYS A CHANCE IT
MAY BE ON.

BALCONIES ARE NOT SAFE PLACES TO PLAY.

STAY AWAY FROM OPEN WINDOWS.

DO NOT PUT ANYTHING IN ELECTRICAL OUTLETS.

DO NOT TOUCH ANY MEDICINE
UNLESS A GROWNUP GIVES IT TO
YOU.